THE ORIGINAL COWGIRL

THE WILD ADVENTURES OF LUCILLE MULHALL

by
HEATHER LANG

pictures by
SUZANNE BEAKY

ALBERT WHITMAN & COMPANY
CHICAGO, ILLINOIS

Lucille wasn't like most girls in the 1890s. Instead of skipping with her mama's clothesline, she twirled it like a lasso. *Whoosh…whoosh…snap!* Lucille could rope a fence post in three seconds flat.

Lucille's papa, Colonel Zack Mulhall, saw right away she could be a mighty fine ranch hand.

Her mama did not. Roping and riding were not ladylike.

Lucille didn't care about sewing or cooking or becoming a lady. Ladies rode sidesaddle, and riding sidesaddle was slower than a snail climbing a greased log.

Lucille wore a split skirt, and she rode astride, just like the cowboys.

By the time she was ten, Lucille was mending fences, training racehorses, and herding cattle.

Lucille swung her lariat at jackrabbits and chickens. The family dogs had to watch their tails when Lucille was around.

During the spring roundup, Lucille asked her papa, "When can I have my own herd?"

"When you're old enough to rope and brand your own cattle," he said.

Colonel Mulhall soon discovered she already could.

Lucille's mama worried about her a lot. The pastures were filled with longhorns, wolves, and coyotes so mean they could turn the strongest cowboy into buzzard food.

Wild animals didn't scare Lucille. When a wolf was
killing her calves, she rode out to search for him. She
spotted the vicious varmint eating in the pasture and
charged with her lariat swinging. *Whoosh…whoosh…snap.*
The wolf put up a ferocious fight, but he was no match
for Lucille.

The only thing that scared Lucille was not being able to ride and rope, so she always hid her scrapes and bruises from her mama.

One day she roped an unbroken horse in the pasture, and it pulled her clear out of her saddle. Tangled up in the lariat, Lucille bounced behind the galloping horse. Finally she cut herself free.

When Lucille was thirteen, her papa organized some rough-riding and roping competitions for his cowboys. Lucky for Lucille, he invited her to come along.

She stuck like a burr to her galloping pony, and with a gentle flick of her wrist, her rope sang for the crowd. Newspapers praised Lucille, the daring young girl who "held the audience in a breathless spell" and was "the envy of half the men." Folks had never seen such a fearless girl.

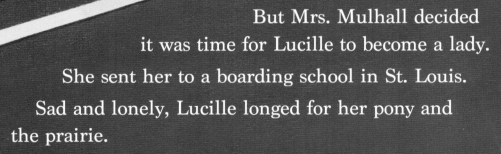

But Mrs. Mulhall decided
it was time for Lucille to become a lady.

She sent her to a boarding school in St. Louis.

Sad and lonely, Lucille longed for her pony and
the prairie.

At the end of the term, her papa welcomed her home
with a beautiful sixteen-hand chestnut horse. Governor was
smart and sweeter than a lump of sugar. Lucille knew right
away she could train him to be a sensational trick horse.

That summer, a committee invited Colonel Mulhall and his cowboys to entertain Vice Presidential candidate Teddy Roosevelt in Oklahoma City. They asked Lucille to show off her roping and riding skills.

Mrs. Mulhall shook her head. "I don't wish my girls to be tomboys."

The committee begged. It was unpatriotic to say no.

Lucille pleaded.

At last Mrs. Mulhall agreed, but on one condition: it would be Lucille's last appearance.

In front of 25,000 spectators, Lucille made the most of it.

Roosevelt bowed to Lucille and told her she was as good as any of his Rough Riders. "Zack, before that girl dies or gets married or cuts up some other caper, you ought to put her on the stage and let the world see what she can do. She's simply great!" Roosevelt insisted.

Colonel Mulhall reckoned it was a fine idea.

And Mrs. Mulhall couldn't stop them.

Was the world ready for a girl cowboy?

Traveling around the country, Lucille thrilled crowds with her daring acts.

From El Paso to St. Louis to New York, newspapers spread the word about Lucille Mulhall—the golden-haired gal who "weighs only ninety pounds, but can break a bronco, lasso and brand a steer, and shoot a coyote at fifty yards."

El Paso

New York

St. Louis

Some folks thought
she was plumb crazy.
In most states women
couldn't even vote or
own property.

She thought *they*
were the crazy ones.

"I feel sorry for the girls who
have to attend so many teas and be
indoors so much," she said.

Lucille raced against cowboys, rode wild broncos, and performed tricks with Governor.

She roped five galloping cowboys all at once.

Reporters hounded her for interviews.

"Aren't you afraid your horse will slip and fall?" a reporter asked.

"Oh, I expect that," Lucille answered. "I'm not afraid of getting hurt."

Lucille preferred to spend her time roping and riding and performing—not talking about it.

When Lucille was fifteen, she entered her first professional steer-roping competition.

Some men laughed at her. A woman roping and tying 1200 pound steers?

Some made bets against her. No other woman had ever competed against men in a professional steer-roping contest.

Lucille didn't give a lick about what people thought.

She steadied her horse.

The steer charged out of the pen.

Lucille took off in hot pursuit, swinging her lariat.

Her first throw landed over the steer's giant horns.

But the rope broke and the steer escaped.

Quick as a jackrabbit she spun another rope.

Whoosh…whoosh…snap! The loop settled around the beast's horns.

Then she flipped him up like a flapjack.

In a flash she jumped off her horse, and with two wraps and a hooey, she tied the steer's feet...29 ½ seconds.

Faster than any of the men!

Soon Lucille broke the world record for steer roping. Cowboys and folks all over the world cheered for the woman who roped and rode better than a man.

Other folks still believed Lucille belonged in the home, not on a horse. But her home was always on a horse with the sun on her cheeks, a lariat coiled in her hand, and the boundless Oklahoma prairie rolling out in front of her.

MORE ABOUT LUCILLE MULHALL

Lucille Mulhall wasn't just a fearless roper and rider; she dared to be an equal to men at a time when the world considered women "the weaker sex." At the turn of the nineteenth century, most rodeos refused to let women compete. Women were expected to act like ladies. Some women risked jail if they rode astride and wore anything unconventional like a split skirt.

Life on the frontier was harsh, and injuries were inevitable for ranch hands, roughriders, and steer ropers. Lucille had many injuries, sometimes during

shows. In 1902 she seriously injured her leg when a rider and horse trampled her during a relay race. The doctors thought she would never ride again, but Lucille was back in saddle in 1903, performing and winning contests.

Despite her tough and spunky spirit, Lucille was soft-spoken and modest. She did not like to brag or talk about herself. She believed in using "patience, perseverance, and gentleness" to train her horses, not whips. Lucille trained her trick horse Governor to perform over forty tricks. Crowds went wild when he rang a dinner bell, played dead, and walked on his knees.

TIMELINE

1885: Lucille is born on October 21 in St. Louis, Missouri.

1889: Zack Mulhall rides in the Oklahoma land run and stakes claim to 80,000 acres in Alfred, Oklahoma, and the Mulhall family settles there.

1899: Zack Mulhall organizes Lucille and local cowboys to form the Congress of Rough Riders and Ropers. They give exhibitions in nearby towns and at the St. Louis World's Fair.

1900: The Congress of Rough Riders and Ropers perform for Teddy Roosevelt in Oklahoma City. Roosevelt is so impressed by Lucille, he invites the Mulhalls to a private dinner.

At first people were suspicious about a woman competing in professional steer roping. When Lucille won her first contest, folks swarmed her from the grandstands. They pulled at her hair and tugged at her clothes. They thought she must be a man pretending to be a woman.

Lucille often won the top prize money in steer-roping contests. Her many admirers included Teddy Roosevelt, Apache Chief Geronimo, and the famous cowboy and comedian Will Rogers. She earned nicknames like "Queen of the Range," "Queen of the Rough Riders," "World's Greatest Horsewoman," "the Cowpuncher Queen," and "America's First Cowgirl." Folks say the term "cowgirl" became popular because of Lucille. She set the stage for other cowgirls to pursue their dreams. These cowgirls spoke highly of Lucille, claiming she was never jealous and always helped others, even her competition.

Lucille's motives were simple. She loved roping and riding and she persisted in doing them, despite the challenges and dangers. More importantly she didn't care what people thought. By following her passion she became an example for cowgirls, female athletes, and women all over the world.

1901: The Mulhall Wild West Show travels on trains from state to state and Lucille is the star.

1905: Lucille leads a parade up Fifth Avenue in New York and performs at Madison Square Garden.

1917: Lucille retires from traveling. Wild West shows lose profitability after the United States enters World War I and Hollywood Westerns become popular.

1903: Lucille beats the best ropers in the West, tying a steer in thirty seconds. She also wins the top $1,000 prize, roping three steers in a total of two minutes and thirty-four seconds.

1913: Lucille starts her own troupe and later becomes the first woman to produce a rodeo when she creates Lucille Mulhall's Roundup.

1940: Lucille dies on December 21.

ACKNOWLEDGMENTS

A special thanks to author and historian Glenda Riley and Lucille's granddaughter, Beverly Van Bergen, for their insights into Lucille and the Wild West. I am also grateful to Debra Osborne Spindle at the Oklahoma Historical Society and Lisa Chassaing at the Monastery of the Visitation for providing valuable research assistance.

For Dad—**HL**

To Matt, my husband and best friend—**SB**

Library of Congress Cataloging-in-Publication
Data is on file with the publisher.

The design is by Jordan Kost.

For more information about Albert Whitman & Company,
visit our web site at www.albertwhitman.com